Collins

easy learning

Starting school workbook

Ages 3–5

Carol Medcalf

How to use this book

This book is designed to help your child become better prepared for school and can be used during the reception year. It focuses on all seven areas of development required in school, increasing in difficulty as your child works through the book to challenge and extend your child's knowledge and skills.

- Find a quiet, comfortable place to work, away from distractions.

- Activities in each subject get increasingly harder as you work through the book, so work through in order spending time on suggested further activities before moving on.

- Help with reading the instructions where necessary and ensure that your child understands what to do.

- When questions have two parts, it is often best to gain the first answer and record it before moving on to the next part of the question.

- If an activity is too difficult for your child then do more of our suggested practical activities (see Parent's tip) and return to the page when you know that they're likely to achieve it.

- Always end each activity before your child gets tired so that they will be eager to return next time. Judge carefully their mood to make this a positive experience. Learning should be fun and not forced.

- Help and encourage your child to check their own answers as they complete each activity. If your child gives an incorrect answer, try to avoid saying that it is wrong, instead ask them to check their own answer carefully so they spot the mistake.

- Let your child return to their favourite pages once they have been completed. Talk about the activities they enjoyed and what they have learnt.

Special features of this book:

- **Parent's tip:** situated at the bottom of every left-hand page, this suggests further activities and encourages discussion about what your child has learnt.

- **Progress panel:** situated at the bottom of every right-hand page, the smiley faces help your child to process how they feel about the page and their achievements.

  Here's a key to help explain what the faces represent:

  🙁 I feel uncertain/I don't understand yet

  😐 I feel OK/I need more practice

  🙂 I feel happy/I fully understand

  It is important that they are building confidence in their abilities and feel good about themselves.

- **Certificate:** the certificate on the inside back cover should be used to reward your child for their effort and achievement. Remember to give them plenty of praise and encouragement, regardless of how they do.

All the activities in this book reflect the goals of the Department of Education's 'Development Matters in the Early Years Foundation Stage (EYFS)'. Your child's nursery or school will be teaching the subjects found in these seven areas of learning and development of the EYFS.

This table shows which pages of this book focus on which areas of learning and development:

Area of Learning and Development	Aspect	Pages
Personal, Social and Emotional Development	Making relationships	Pages 4, 5
	Self-confidence and self-awareness	
	Managing feelings and behaviour	
Physical Development	Moving and handling	Pages 6–9
	Health and self-care	
Communication and Language	Listening and attention	Pages 10, 11
	Understanding	
	Speaking	
Literacy	Reading	Pages 12–17
	Writing	
Mathematics	Numbers	Pages 18–23
	Shape, space and measure	
Understanding the World	People and communities	Pages 24–31
	The world	
	Technology	
Expressive Arts and Design	Exploring and using media and materials	Pages 4, 9
	Being imaginative	

Published by Collins
An imprint of HarperCollins*Publishers* Ltd
The News Building
1 London Bridge Street
London
SE1 9GF

Browse the complete Collins catalogue at www.collins.co.uk

© HarperCollins*Publishers* Ltd 2013
This edition © HarperCollins*Publishers* Ltd 2015

15 14 13 12

ISBN 978-0-00-815160-7

The author asserts the moral right to be identified as the author of this work.

British Library Cataloguing in Publication Data.

A Catalogue record for this publication is available from the British Library.

Written by Carol Medcalf
Page layout by Linda Miles, Lodestone Publishing and Contentra Technologies Ltd
Illustrated by Jenny Tulip
Cover design by Sarah Duxbury and Paul Oates
Cover illustration by John Haslam
Project managed by Chantal Peacock and Sonia Dawkins

Printed in Great Britain by Martins the Printers

Contents

About me

- Colour the following to match you.

My hair is

My eyes are

My skin is

- Can you add features on this face to make it look like you?

Children need to feel good about their own identity and understand that we are all different and unique. Understanding their own feelings and those of others around them is very important and will help with social skills.

Feelings

happy   sad   angry   surprised

● Draw on the faces below.

How do you feel today?

How does a member of your family feel today?

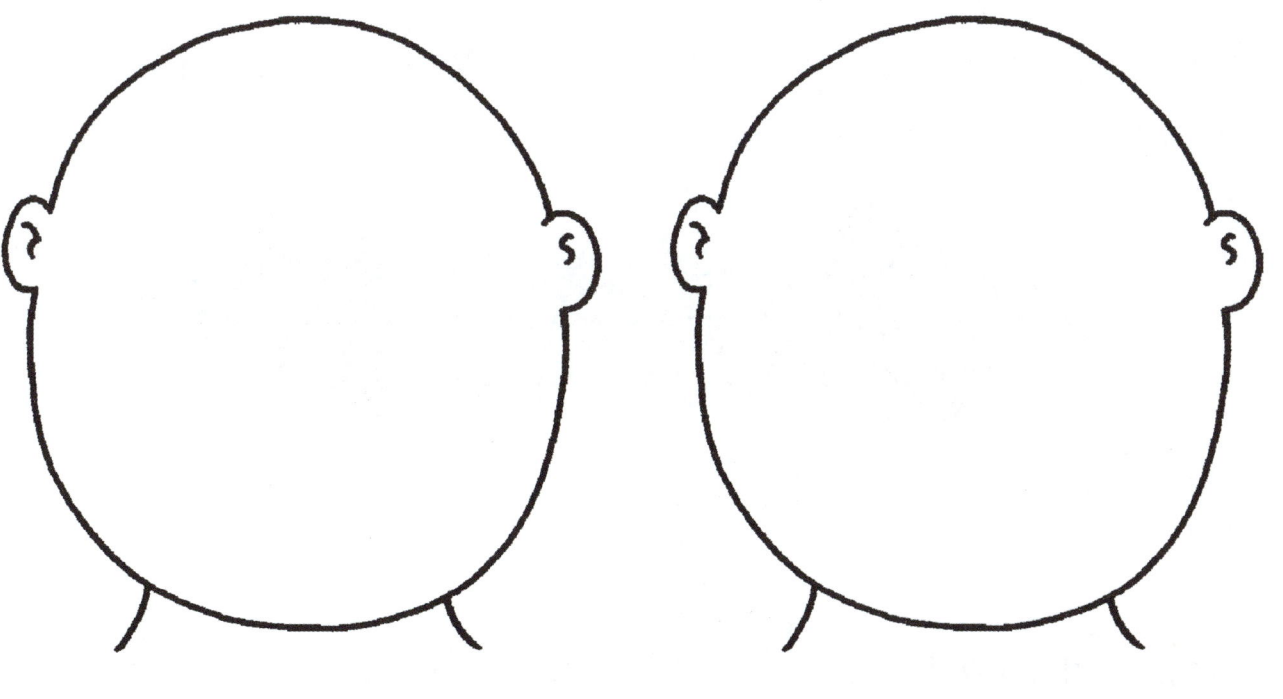

How do you feel about these pages? Tick ✔ the box next to the face that shows how you feel.

Positional words

- Look at the group of children playing below.

Colour the t-shirts in the statements below to match the picture.

The child with the  t-shirt is at the **front**.

The child with the t-shirt is **behind** the rest.

- Now look at this picture and colour the t-shirts in the statements below.

The child with the t-shirt is **first**.

The child with the t-shirt is **last**.

Animal circus

- Look at the lions below.
  Draw a circle ◯ round the lion that is **on** the box.
  Cross ✗ out the lion that is **under** the table.

- Look at the circus below.
  Draw a circle ◯ round the monkey who is **beside** the elephant.
  Cross ✗ out the monkey who is **inside** the box.

How do you feel about these pages? Tick ✔ the box next to the face that shows how you feel.

 ☐ ☐ ☐

Story time

The pictures below show a story. Can you look at the pictures and tell someone the story? Here are some ideas to get you started...

What could you call the story?

What are the children's names?

What is the weather like?

After your child has told you the stories on these pages, discuss the stories with them. For example, 'I wonder what happened?', 'who did it happen to?' or 'how do you think it happened?'

Can you draw your own pictures below to tell a story? Draw the pictures then tell someone all about what you have drawn.

1

2

3

4

How do you feel about these pages? Tick ✔ the box next to the face that shows how you feel.

 ☐   ☐   ☐

Staying safe

- Look at these pictures. Can you spot anything happening that is dangerous? Draw a circle ◯ round the things that you find.

- Look at these signs. They all help you to avoid danger. When you go out, see if you can spot them. Tick ✔ them when you have seen them and know what they mean.

Ask your child what they would do in the situations above and talk about safety. It is never too early to have a fire escape plan at home and have a fire drill. Make sure your child would know what to do in an emergency such as a fire or accident at home.

Healthy eating

• Below are two big, empty plates. Can you cut out some pictures from old magazines, leaflets or catalogues and stick them into two groups on the plates?

Healthy food – we can eat lots of this type of food.

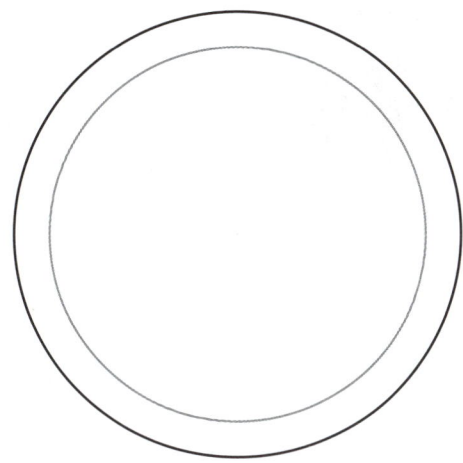

Un-healthy food – we can only eat these foods in small amounts as they are not as good for us.

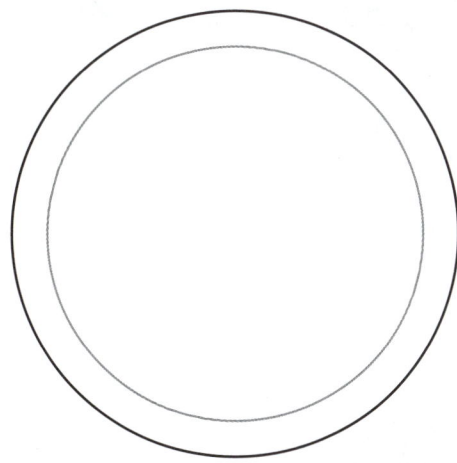

How do you feel about these pages? Tick ✔ the box next to the face that shows how you feel.

The alphabet

● Join the dots to write the alphabet. Can you say all the sounds for these letters?

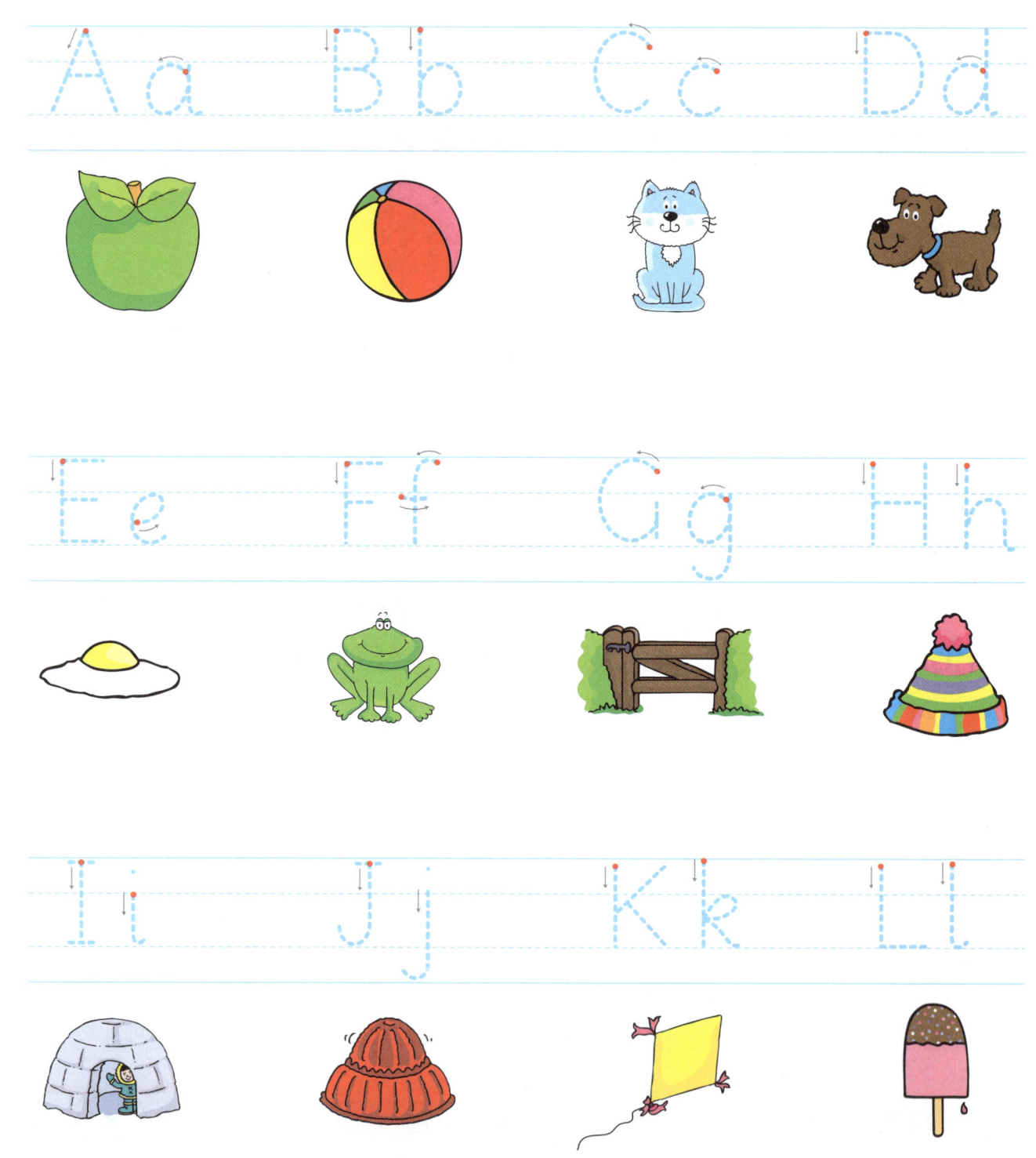

As you work through these pages, reinforce the phonetic sounds of each letter. This will help later on when your child is learning to read words by sounding out letters.

M m   N n   O o   P p

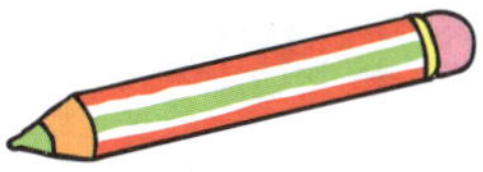

Q q   R r   S s   T t

U u   V v   W w   X x

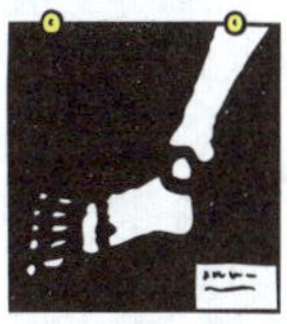

Y y   Z z

How do you feel about these pages? Tick ✔ the box next to the face that shows how you feel.

 ☐   ☐   ☐

Drawing patterns

● Join the dots in this picture. Can you see any patterns that look like letters?

When writing the high-frequency words (words that appear often in writing), read them with your child. These words cannot be said phonetically like other simple words that they have been learning so it is important that they can recognise these words.

High-frequency words

Some words appear quite often when you are reading, such as the ones below. Read these words with the person helping you and join the dots to write them.

I   I   up   up

look   look   we   we

like   like   and   and

on   on   at   at

for   for   is   is

How do you feel about these pages? Tick ✔ the box next to the face that shows how you feel.

Four-letter words

● Which letters do the following words start with? Write the letter on the line and cross ✗ out the one that is wrong.

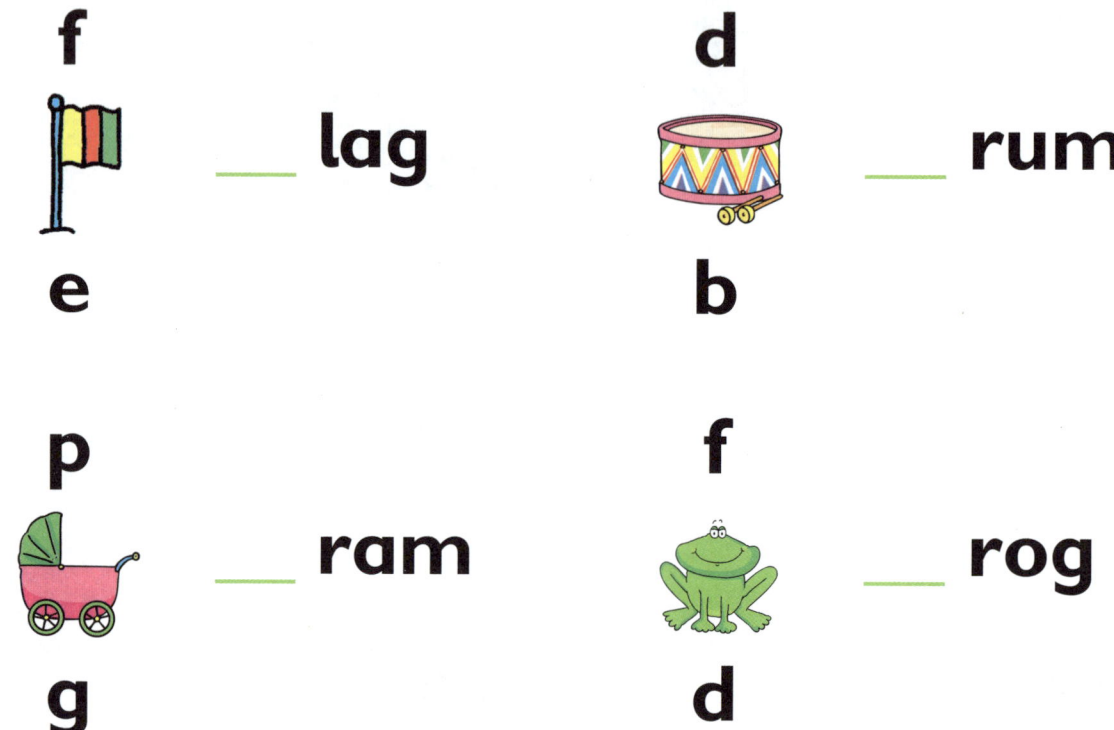

f

_ lag

e

d

_ rum

b

p

_ ram

g

f

_ rog

d

● Draw a line to match these words to the right picture.

crab

doll

fish

door

● Draw lines to match the words to the pictures.

trap

milk

swim

crab

slug

plug

hand

club

glug

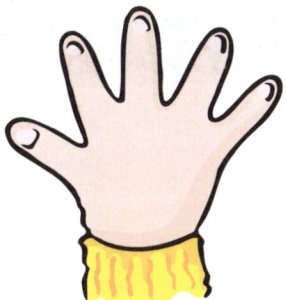

tent

drop

flag

stop

nest

flop

Number puzzle

● Look at the numbers on the lorry.
How many of each of the numbers below can you
find? Count each number in turn slowly. It may help
to cross them out as you find them.

0 _____   1 _____   2 _____   3 _____   4 _____   5 _____

● Write the number that comes next in each row.

1 2 3 _____   2 3 4 _____

4 5 6 _____   0 1 2 _____

5 6 7 _____   6 7 8 _____

Look at the chart. Colour the squares on the graph to show the correct number of animals.

Write the number that comes first in each row.

_____ 2 3 4   _____ 5 6 7

_____ 4 5 6   _____ 7 8 9

_____ 1 2 3   _____ 8 9 10

How do you feel about these pages? Tick ✔ the box next to the face that shows how you feel.

 ☐   ☐   ☐

Counting

- Look at these pictures.

  How many horses are in the field?
  How many horses are in the stable?

How many spiders are in the web?
How many spiders are hanging on the branch?

● Circle the correct number to match the picture.

There are 10, 3, 8 jellyfish.

There are 3, 4, 6 turtles.

There are 5, 7, 9 fish.

● Look at the bottles below. Can you fill in the missing numbers on the bottles?

Measurement

● Look at these flowers. Can you write how tall each flower is in the green boxes?

  Colour the tallest flower pink.

  Colour the shortest flower yellow.

● Now can you measure these snakes? Write the answers in each green box.

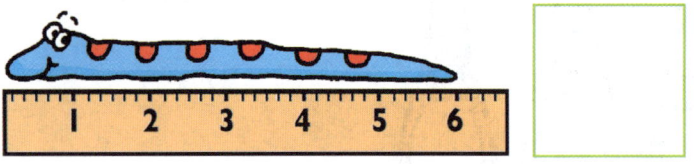 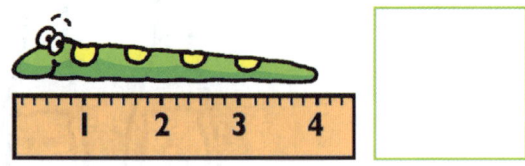

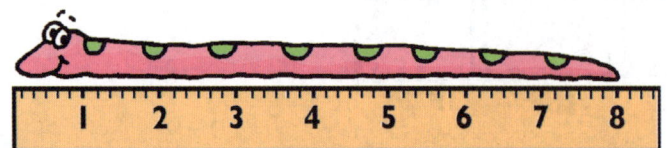  

Measure the height of your child regularly by putting a long piece of paper or card on a wall to plot their height. It is a lovely record to keep and shows them how they are growing as well as providing an excellent opportunity to learn about measurement.

3D shapes

- These are all 3D shapes, can you colour them?

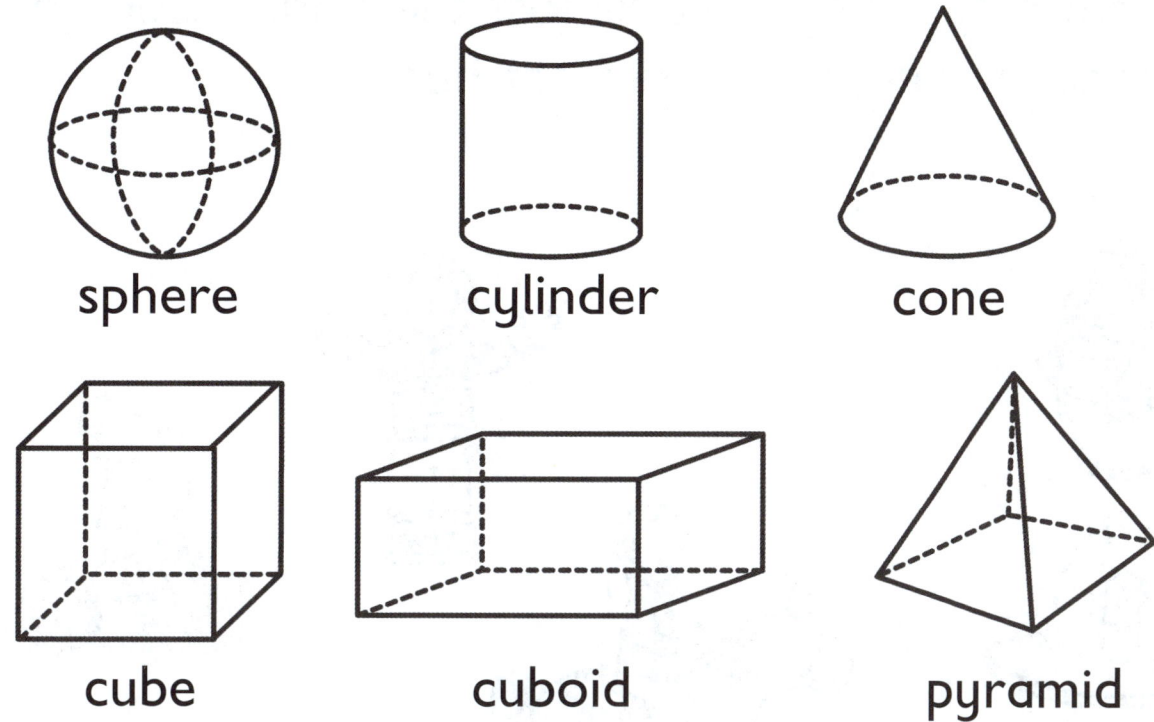

sphere   cylinder   cone

cube   cuboid   pyramid

- Look at these pictures. Can you match the 3D shape to the object that is the same shape?

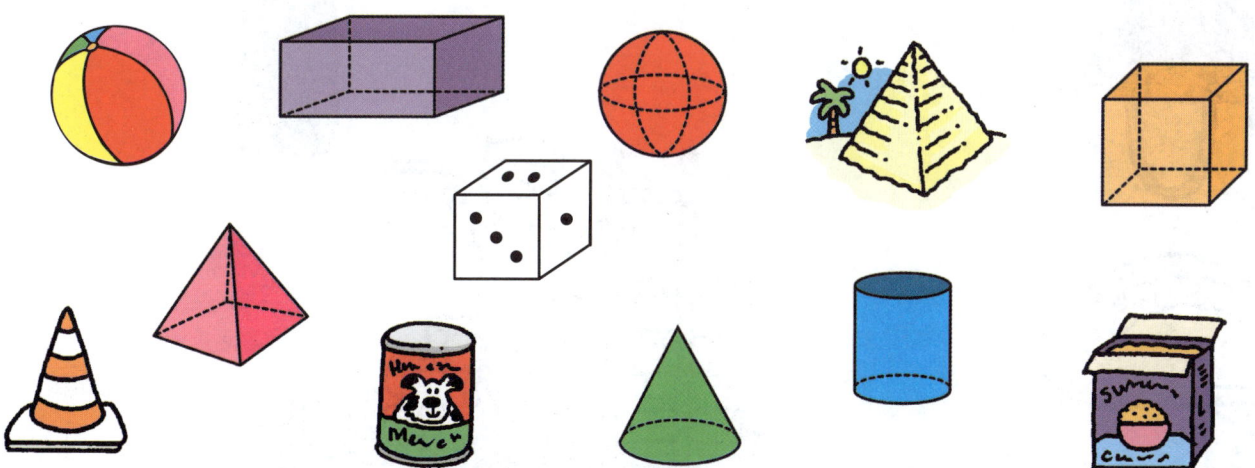

How do you feel about these pages? Tick ✔ the box next to the face that shows how you feel.

 ☐   ☐   ☐

Hats

- These are people that you may see out in your community. They have all lost their hats. Can you match the people to the right hats?

It is important for children to learn that we are not all the same and that other families may have different values and customs to our own. Read up with your child about other people and their religions and customs.

Religion and festivals

There are lots of different religions around the world who celebrate festivals to mark special occasions in their religious calendars.

- Colour and talk about the pictures celebrating different festivals.

Christian

Jewish

Hindu

Muslim

How do you feel about these pages? Tick ✔ the box next to the face that shows how you feel.

Space

There are 8 planets in our solar system. We live on planet Earth.

● Look at the picture of our solar system and count the planets. Colour the Sun and all the planets. Can you circle Earth?

Space is an excellent way to introduce counting backwards – '10, 9, 8, 7, 6, 5, 4, 3, 2, 1, 0, blast off!' Extend as your child achieves these numbers by starting from 20. Look at numbers counting down on the microwave and change 'blast off' for 'cooked'!

We send rockets into space to explore the solar system.

● Can you find the rocket and cross it out?

Jupiter   Saturn   Uranus   Neptune

How do you feel about these pages? Tick ✔ the box next to the face that shows how you feel.

Transport

There are lots of different ways for us to travel and move around.

- Colour the different types of transport and tick ✔ the box if you have travelled that way.

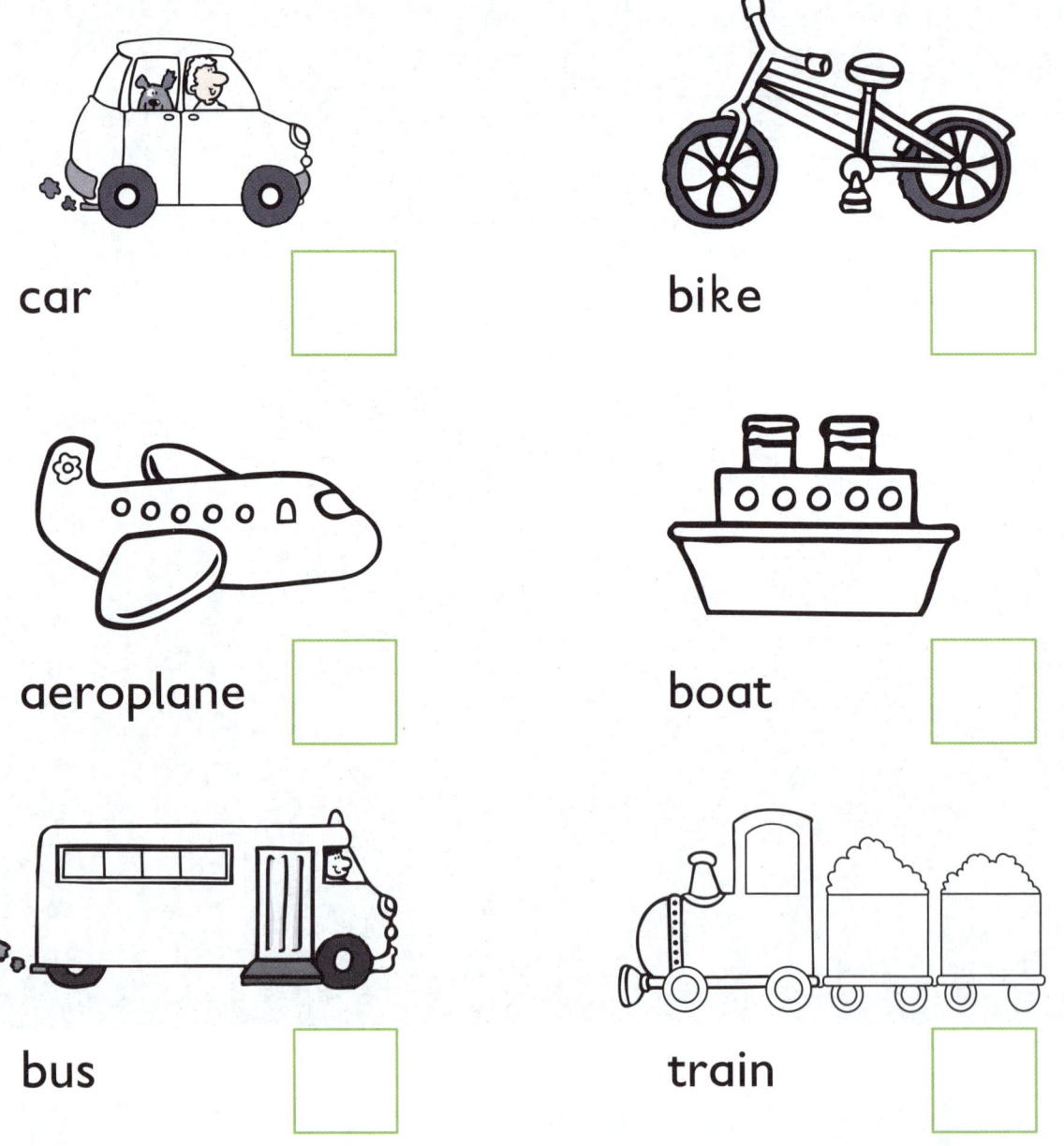

car ☐

bike ☐

aeroplane ☐

boat ☐

bus ☐

train ☐

Further this activity on transport by discussing which way you think would be the fastest or slowest way to travel. Talk about how to get to another country close or far away to where you live. What transport would you use? Would you need to use more than one type of transport?

- Here are some more unusual ways to travel.
  Tick ✔ the box if you have ever travelled this way.

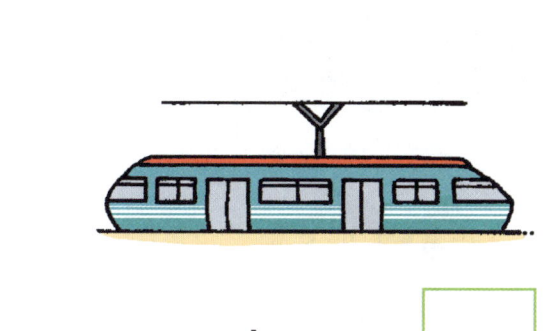

hot air balloon ☐

cable car ☐

tram ☐

helicopter ☐

You may also travel by walking. ☐

- Look back at all the ways to travel on these two pages.
  Circle ◯ which way you travel the most.
  Put a cross ✘ by all the transport that has wheels.

Growing and changing

All living things grow and change as time moves on.

- Can you put the pictures in order? Write 1, 2, 3 and 4 in the green boxes.

- Can you put the pictures in order? Write 1, 2, 3 and 4 in the green boxes.

An early learning goal is for children to be able to operate simple computer equipment and use a range of technology to understand how things work. Extend by talking about how some things use remote controls.

Technology

- Look at the pictures below. How do the items work? Can you draw lines to match the items to either the plug or batteries?

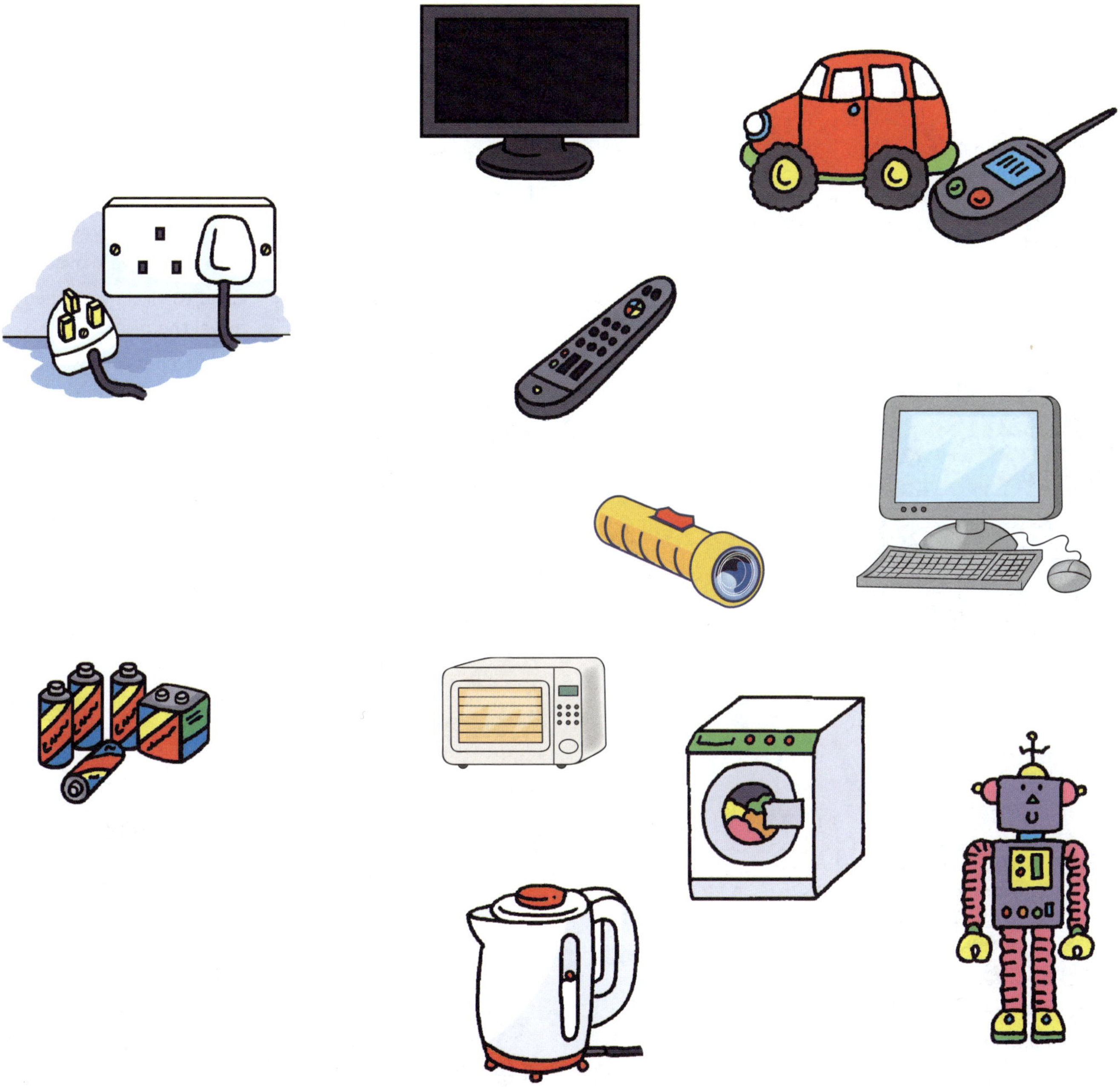

How do you feel about these pages? Tick ✔ the box next to the face that shows how you feel.

31

Answers

Page 4
Child to colour hair, eyes and skin

Child to add their own features to the face

Page 5
Child to draw features on the faces

Page 6
The child with the  t-shirt is at the front

The child with the  t-shirt is behind the rest

The child with the  t-shirt is first

The child with the  t-shirt is last

Page 7

Page 8
Child to tell story

Page 9
Child to draw story

Page 10

Child to tick signs they have seen and understood

Page 11
Child to stick pictures of food on plates

Page 12
Child to join the dots

Page 13
Child to join the dots

Page 14
Child to join the dots

Page 15
Child to join the dots

Page 16
f | f_ lag
d | d_ rum
p | p_ ram
f | f_ rog

crab
doll
fish
door

Page 17
trap
milk
swim

hand
club
glug

stop
nest
flop

crab
slug
plug

tent
drop
flag

Page 18
0 1 1 3 2 4 3 1 4 1 5 3
1 2 3 4   2 3 4 5
4 5 6 7   0 1 2 3
5 6 7 8   6 7 8 9

Page 19

Page 20

1   1
3   5

Page 21
There are 10, 3, 8 jellyfish
There are 3, 4, 6 turtles
There are 5, 7, 9 fish

0 1 2 3 4 5
6 7 8 9 10

Page 22
7   5   3
6   4
8   1

Page 23
Child to colour shapes

Page 24

Page 25
Child to colour pictures

Page 26
Child to colour planets and circle Earth

Page 27
Child to colour planets and cross out rocket

Page 28
Child to colour transport and tick boxes showing how they have travelled

Page 29
Child to tick boxes showing how they have travelled

Child to circle way they travel the most

Child to put a cross by car, bike, bus and train

Page 30

2   1
3   4
4   1
3   2

Page 31
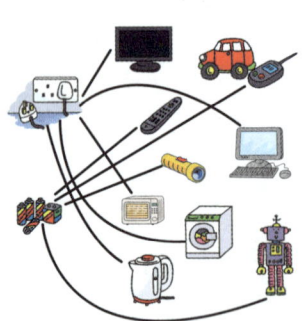

1234   4567
3456   6789
0123   78910